Affiliate Marketing Handbook

Build a Successful Online Business and Achieve Financial Freedom

WILL STRONG

Table of Contents

Introduction

You did it! Congratulations, you've taken the first step towards harnessing the full power of affiliate marketing and securing financial freedom. With this book, you will learn the ins and outs of affiliate marketing and how it can truly change your life. The flexibility of affiliate marketing allows you to invest as much or as little time as you desire, with the added incentive of proportional rewards for the effort you put in. Whether you choose to pursue affiliate marketing as a side hustle while maintaining your full-time job or fully immerse yourself in the thrilling world of affiliate marketing, the possibilities are endless. So, let's get started!

First of all, I want to thank you for choosing my book to help guide you on your journey. It really means a lot. I sincerely hope you find the information between these pages useful whether you're new to affiliate marketing or a marketing veteran in need of a little refresher. I'm confident that armed with the information I impart in this book along with a bit of patience, dedication and persistence, you'll be well on your way to becoming a successful affiliate marketer in no time. Affiliate marketing done right can be very lucrative, creating freedom and wealth for you and your family in a way that you may not have deemed possible before.

I've been involved in affiliate marketing for over 10 years and seen first-hand just how life changing it can be. When I first started out, I didn't have a clue what I was doing. I just knew I had to learn about this seemingly magical way to earn money online. I stumbled through at first like a toddler trying to take his first steps, but after 10 years of blood, sweat and tears in the game, I can look back and see exactly where I was going wrong and what I should have done differently. And that's part of my motivation for writing this book. I want to impart all the valuable knowledge that I've learned over the years in the hope that it can help someone like you. Help you avoid the mistakes I made and help you succeed first time round, saving you valuable time and effort.

I have written this book in such a way that it would have been exactly the type of book I wish I had all those years ago when I was first starting out. You can think of it as your little companion, always there to help you out and reference whenever needed on your journey to making money online as an affiliate marketer. I have intentionally arranged the different sections in such a way that things are laid out in steps and bullet points. I find this format to be a lot easier to digest and reference back to later. Also, I believe it's helpful to have things laid out in steps and bullet points to make the information more actionable. It's no use in discussing the theory of affiliate marketing and potential of making money online all day without following through. Action is what's needed!

Within these pages, you'll find logical, actionable steps to ensure you've got something to be getting stuck into straightaway. However, I do recommend reading through this book to the end first and then going back to the steps outlines and implementing them one at a time. That way you can gain solid understanding of the type of journey you're embarking on before you get started. This will ensure that you have the best possible chance of succeeding.

Are you ready to start this exciting journey and discover the awesome money-making power of affiliate marketing? Then let's get into it. As Lao Tzu once said "A journey of a thousand miles begins with a single step"

Affiliate Marketing 101

What is Affiliate Marketing?

Affiliate marketing is a type of performance-based marketing where a business rewards affiliates for each customer brought about by the affiliate's own marketing efforts. It is an online marketing strategy in which a business partners with affiliates, who promote the business's products or services to their own audiences.

In affiliate marketing, the affiliate earns a commission for each sale or lead generated as a result of their promotional efforts. The commission is a percentage of the sale price, or a flat fee for each lead generated. The affiliate does not purchase or own the product or service they promote, but instead earns a commission for every successful sale or lead.

Affiliate marketing provides a cost-effective way for businesses to reach new customers and expand their reach. The business only pays the affiliate when a sale or lead is generated, so there is no upfront cost to the business. It also allows businesses to tap into the audiences of their affiliates, giving them access to new and potentially untapped markets.

Affiliates, on the other hand, benefit from being able to promote products or services they believe in and earn a commission for doing so. Affiliate marketing is also an attractive option for those looking to start their own online business, as it requires minimal investment and offers the potential for significant earnings.

Overall, affiliate marketing is a win-win scenario for both businesses and affiliates. Businesses gain access to new audiences and affiliates can earn income through promoting products and services they believe in. With the rise of e-commerce and online marketing, affiliate marketing has become a popular and lucrative industry for those looking to start or grow their own online business. You couldn't be starting at a better time!

Benefits of Affiliate Marketing

Turning to making money online has become increasingly popular in recent years, and affiliate marketing is one of the most accessible ways to do so. In this performance-based marketing strategy, you can earn money by promoting products or services to your own audience, making it an attractive option for those looking to start or grow an online business.

So, what exactly are the benefits of making money online with affiliate marketing in particular? Let's take a closer look.

1. **Flexibility:** One of the biggest benefits of affiliate marketing is the flexibility it provides. You can work from anywhere, at any time, and have the freedom to set your own schedule. This is particularly beneficial for those who have other commitments, such as a full-time job or family commitments. The flexible nature of affiliate marketing also allows you to travel and work from pretty much anywhere, provided you have access to a laptop and a WI-FI signal of course.

2. **Low Investment:** Starting an affiliate marketing business requires minimal investment, making it a low-risk option for those looking to start their own online business. All you need is a website or social media platform, and you're good to go!

3. **Potential for High Earnings:** As an affiliate marketer, you can earn a commission for each sale or lead you bring in. The commission is often a percentage of the sale price or a flat fee, providing you with the potential to earn a significant amount of money especially with high ticket items.

4. **Promote Products You Believe In:** One of the best things about affiliate marketing is that you get to choose what products or services you want to promote. This allows you to align your personal values with your work, leading to increased satisfaction and a more positive work experience.

5. **Learn More as You Go:** As an affiliate marketer, you will have the opportunity to learn bucket loads about online marketing strategies, including SEO, social media marketing, and email marketing. This can help you to improve your marketing skills and expand your knowledge, making you a more well-rounded online marketer.

6. **Unlimited Earning Potential:** The beauty of affiliate marketing is that there is no limit to how much you can earn. As you grow your audience and improve your marketing skills, you can increase your earnings, making it a scalable business opportunity. The sky's the limit!

Making money online with affiliate marketing offers numerous benefits for those looking to start their own online business. With its flexibility, low investment, potential for high earnings, and the opportunity to promote products you believe in, affiliate marketing is a smart choice for anyone looking to start or grow an online business. So why not give it a try and start earning money from the comfort of your own home!

How does affiliate marketing work?

Affiliate marketing is a performance-based marketing strategy that allows you to earn money by promoting products or services to your own audience.
Here's a step-by-step breakdown of exactly how affiliate marketing works:

1. **Sign up for an Affiliate Program:** The first step in getting started with affiliate marketing is to sign up for an affiliate program. An affiliate program is a partnership between a merchant and an affiliate, where the affiliate promotes the merchant's products or services and earns a commission for each sale or lead they bring in. A great place to get started is www.clickbank.com. Browse through their affiliate programs to see what best suits you.

2. **Choose Products to Promote:** Once you've signed up for an affiliate program, you can start choosing products or services to promote. It's important to choose products that align with your personal values and interests, as this will make promoting them easier and more enjoyable.

3. **Get Your Unique Affiliate Link:** After you've chosen your products, you'll be given a unique affiliate link. This link is what you'll use to promote the products to your audience. Whenever someone clicks on your affiliate link and makes a purchase, you'll earn a commission for the sale. It's that simple!

4. **Promote Your Affiliate Link:** The next step is to start promoting your affiliate link. This can be done through your website, social media platforms, email marketing, or any other online marketing channels you prefer. The key is to reach your target audience and encourage them to click on your affiliate link.

5. **Earn Commissions:** Whenever someone clicks on your affiliate link and makes a purchase, you'll earn a commission for the sale. The commission is often a percentage of the sale price or a flat fee, and the amount you can earn will vary depending on the affiliate program you're a part of.

That's it! By following these simple steps, you can start earning money with affiliate marketing. It's important to remember that affiliate marketing is a performance-based business, so the more you put into it, the more you'll get out of it. With persistence and hard work, you can turn your affiliate marketing business into a successful and lucrative venture.

Affiliate marketing is a simple, low-risk way to start your own online business and earn money by promoting products you believe in. It's never been more straightforward to earn a living online!

Setting up an affiliate business

Starting an affiliate marketing business can be a great way to turn your passion into a profitable venture. By promoting products or services to people that are seeking to solve a problem they've got, you'll not only be building a lucrative online income, but you'll also be helping people in the process.

When you get started with affiliate marketing, you'll first need to choose a niche that you're passionate about. This could be anything from cooking and food to travel, fashion, or fitness. The more you know about your niche, the easier it will be for you to find products and services to promote and connect with people.

Next, you'll need to build your platform, which could be a website, a blog, a YouTube channel, or a social media account. This will be your space to share your knowledge and promote your affiliate products.

Promoting your affiliate products can be done through your website, social media platforms, email marketing, or any other online marketing channels you prefer. The goal is to reach your target audience and encourage them to click on your affiliate link.

With hard work and persistence, you can turn your affiliate marketing business into a successful and lucrative venture. Whether you're just looking for a side hustle or you want to build a full-time business, affiliate marketing offers the flexibility and low risk you need to get started.

That's a brief outline of what lies ahead. It's a journey that's well worth taking and if done correctly, can be very rewarding indeed. In the next chapter, we'll look at how to understand your target market, an essential step in the affiliate marketing mission.

Understanding Your Target Market

Identifying Your Niche

Finding the right niche for your affiliate marketing business is one of the most important steps to success. Your niche is your area of expertise and it's what sets you apart from others in the industry. Here's how to identify your niche for affiliate marketing:

1. **Identify Your Interests and Passions:** Think about the things you enjoy doing, the topics you love to read about, and the hobbies you have. These are often great starting points for finding your niche.

2. **Look for Problems to Solve:** Your niche should not only be something you're passionate about, but also something where you can add value. Consider the problems people face in your area of interest and think about how you can provide solutions through your affiliate marketing efforts.

3. **Research the Market:** Do some market research to see what niches are already popular and what gaps exist. You want to find a niche that has a good-sized market but isn't already saturated. This will give you the best opportunity to make an impact and stand out.

4. **Evaluate Your Competitors:** Take a look at your competitors and see what they are doing. Look for niches that are under-served or where you have unique insights or knowledge that you can bring to the table.

5. **Narrow Down Your Options:** Once you have a list of potential niches, narrow down your options by evaluating factors such as profitability, market size, competition, and your own strengths.

6. **Choose Your Niche:** Finally, choose the niche that feels right for you. You'll be spending a lot of time and effort on this, so make sure you choose a niche that you're truly passionate about and can see yourself sticking with for the long-term.

By following these steps, you can identify a niche that is both profitable and fulfilling for your affiliate marketing business. When you're passionate about your niche, you'll find it easier to create content, connect with your audience, and promote your products. So, take the time to find your niche and start building a successful affiliate marketing business today!

Researching Your Target Audience

By understanding who your target audience is, you can create content and promotions that will resonate with them and drive conversions. Here's some tips about how to research your target audience:

1. **Define Your Target Audience:** Start by identifying the demographics of your target audience, including their age, gender, income, education, and location. This will give you a general idea of who your audience is and what their interests and needs might be.

2. **Conduct Surveys:** Reach out to your existing audience or potential customers and ask them about their interests, needs, and preferences. This can be done through online surveys, email campaigns, or social media polls.

3. **Analyze Your Competitors' Audience:** Take a look at your competitors and see who they are targeting. This will give you a good idea of who is interested in your niche and what their needs and preferences are.

4. **Utilize Social Media Insights:** Social media platforms like Facebook and Instagram provide valuable insights into your audience, including their demographics and interests. Use these insights to better understand your target audience.

5. **Gather Feedback:** Ask your audience for feedback on your content and promotions. This will give you a better understanding of what they like and don't like and help you make changes to better resonate with them.

6. **Monitor Your Analytics:** Keep an eye on your website and social media analytics to see who is engaging with your content and what types of content are performing well. This will give you a better idea of who your target audience is and what they are looking for.

By researching your target audience, you'll have a better understanding of their needs, preferences, and interests. This will allow you to create content and promotions that will resonate with them and drive conversions. So, take the time to research your target audience and build up a picture of your ideal customers and their needs.

Understanding Consumer Behavior

Now let's have a look at understanding consumer behavior. It involves analyzing how consumers make purchasing decisions and what drives their behavior. This understanding can then be used to create promotions and content that will resonate with the target audience and drive conversions. And ultimately, make more money!

To understand consumer behavior, start by identifying the decision-making process that consumers go through and knowing your target audience's demographics, interests, and preferences. Look at pain points, trends, and motivators to understand what drives consumer behavior. Utilize social proof and consider motivators in your content and promotions.

By keeping consumer behavior in mind, you can create a more effective marketing strategy and increase conversions. It's important to stay up to date on industry trends and consumer behavior trends to continually adjust your strategy and stay ahead of the competition.

It's also important to note that consumer behavior is constantly evolving, so it's crucial to regularly reevaluate and update your understanding of your target audience. One way to do this is to collect data and analyze consumer behavior through tools like surveys, focus groups, and analytics.

Another key aspect of understanding consumer behavior is knowing your competition. Analyze what your competitors are doing and what is working for them and see if you can apply similar strategies to your own affiliate marketing business.

Ultimately, the goal of understanding consumer behavior is to create a customer-centric approach to your affiliate marketing business. By understanding what drives consumer behavior and creating promotions and content that appeals to your target audience, you can build a loyal customer base and increase conversions.

Understanding consumer behavior is important for creating a successful affiliate marketing business. Take the time to understand your target audience and what drives their behavior and use that understanding to create promotions and content that will drive conversions and grow your business to the next level.

Creating Buyer Personas

Creating buyer personas is a critical step in developing a successful affiliate marketing business plan. A buyer persona is a semi-fictional representation of your ideal customer based on market research and data. By creating buyer personas, you can get a better understanding of your target audience and develop a marketing strategy that really resonates with them. Here's what you need to know about creating buyer personas:

1. **Gather Data:** As previously discussed it's important to collect data on your target audience for this step, including demographics, interests, pain points, and decision-making processes. Use this data to create a profile of your ideal customer.

2. **Create a Semi-Fictional Representation:** Use the data you've gathered to create a semi-fictional representation of your ideal customer, including details such as age, occupation, interests, and purchasing habits.

3. **Give Your Persona a Name:** Giving your persona a name helps bring it to life and makes it easier to refer to and remember. It might seem silly, but it really does help to envisage your customer as a real person which will help you to tailor your marketing communications effectively.

4. **Use Your Personas to Guide Your Marketing:** Use your buyer personas to guide your marketing efforts. Consider their interests, pain points, and decision-making processes when creating content and promotions. This will help to really connect with who you're targeting increasing your chances of success.

5. **Regularly Review and Update:** Consumer behavior and preferences can change over time, so it's important to regularly review and update your buyer personas.

By creating buyer personas, you can get a better understanding of your target audience and create a marketing strategy that resonates with them. This leads to increased conversions and a more successful affiliate marketing business. So, take the time to create buyer personas, as it will really help in the long run and avoid creating content that doesn't connect to your audience.

Building an Affiliate Marketing Strategy

Choosing the Right Products to Promote

Choosing the right products to promote is crucial. It's important to carefully consider the products you promote to ensure that they align with your niche and target audience, offer high commission rates, and have a strong sales page. In this section, we'll explore the key factors you should consider when selecting products to promote.

- **Relevance to Your Niche:** When choosing products to promote, it's essential to consider the relevance of the product to your niche. Your target audience should be interested in the product, and it should align with your expertise and interests. For example, if you're in the health and wellness niche, you wouldn't want to promote a product that is not related to health and wellness. By selecting products that are relevant to your niche, you'll increase the chances of your audience being interested in the product and making a purchase.

- **Commission Rates:** Commission rates vary from product to product and from company to company. Look for products with high commission rates as this will increase your earnings and make it easier for you to make a profit from your affiliate marketing efforts. You can find information about commission rates on the product's affiliate program website or by contacting the company directly.

- **Product Quality:** The quality of the product you're promoting is important for several reasons. Firstly, promoting a high-quality product will increase the chances of your audience being satisfied with their purchase. This will lead to increased conversions and a better reputation for you. Secondly, promoting a low-quality product can damage your reputation, leading to decreased trust with your target audience.

- **Sales Page:** The sales page of a product is a crucial component of the customer's decision-making process. A strong sales page will clearly highlight the benefits of the product and provide all the necessary information to make an informed purchase. Look for products with well-designed sales pages that are professional, easy to navigate, and provide a clear call-to-action.

- **Competition:** Consider the level of competition in the market for the product you're considering promoting. If there are many affiliates promoting the same product, it may be more challenging to stand out and drive conversions. In these cases, you may want to consider promoting a product that is not as heavily promoted or find a unique angle to promote the product that sets you apart from other affiliates.

Choosing the right products to promote is an important step in building a successful affiliate marketing business. By considering the relevance to your niche, commission rates, product quality, sales page, and competition, you can increase your chances of success and grow your business. Remember to regularly evaluate your product choices and make changes as necessary to ensure the success of your affiliate marketing efforts.

Selecting Affiliate Networks

An affiliate network acts as an intermediary between you and the companies offering affiliate programs. The right affiliate network will provide access to a wide range of products and services, offer high commission rates, and provide support and resources to help you succeed as an affiliate marketer.

Here are some key factors to consider when selecting an affiliate network:

- **Product Diversity:** Consider the range of products and services offered by the affiliate network. The more products available, the more options you have for promoting products that align with your niche and target audience. Consider the quality of the products, the commission rates offered, and the sales pages of the products.

- **Commission Rates:** Commission rates can vary greatly between affiliate networks and products. Look for affiliate networks that offer high commission rates, as this will help increase your earnings. Commission rates can also vary based on the type of product you're promoting, so be sure to research the different products available before joining an affiliate network.

- **Reputation:** The reputation of the affiliate network is important because it will impact your ability to earn money and build trust with your audience. Look for affiliate networks with a strong reputation and a history of paying affiliates on time. Research the network's reviews, testimonials, and ratings to get a better understanding of its reputation.

- **Support:** Consider the level of support provided by the affiliate network. Look for affiliate networks that offer resources, such as training and tutorials, to help you succeed. A good affiliate network should also provide customer support and respond promptly to any questions or issues you may have.

- **Payment Options:** Make sure the affiliate network provides payment options that work for you. Look for affiliate networks that offer multiple payment options, such as direct deposit or PayPal, to make it easy for you to receive your earnings. Consider the payment frequency and terms, such as the minimum payment threshold and payment processing time.

- **Tracking and Reporting:** The ability to accurately track and report your earnings is critical to your success as an affiliate marketer. Look for affiliate networks that provide robust tracking and reporting tools, so you can see exactly how much you're earning and track your progress. Consider the level of detail provided in the tracking and reporting tools, such as the number of clicks, conversions, and sales.

Selecting the right affiliate network is an important step in building a successful affiliate marketing business. Consider the product diversity, commission rates, reputation, support, payment options, and tracking and reporting tools offered by the affiliate network. Research the different affiliate networks available and make an informed decision based on your specific needs and goals. The right affiliate network will provide you with the resources and support you need to succeed as an affiliate marketer.

Here's a list of the top affiliate networks out there now with good reputations and solid useability:

1. **Amazon Associates:** Amazon Associates is one of the largest and most established affiliate networks. It offers a wide range of products in various categories, making it easy for affiliates to find a product that fits their niche. Additionally, Amazon offers a generous commission rate and provides detailed analytics, making it easy for affiliates to track their performance.

2. **Commission Junction:** Commission Junction is another popular affiliate network that offers a wide range of products and a competitive commission structure. It also provides comprehensive reporting and tracking tools, making it easy for affiliates to see how their campaigns are performing.

3. **ShareASale:** ShareASale is a user-friendly affiliate network that offers a wide range of products, a competitive commission structure, and excellent customer support. It also provides detailed analytics, making it easy for affiliates to monitor their campaigns and optimize their performance.

4. **Rakuten Marketing:** Rakuten Marketing is a leading affiliate network that offers a wide range of products, competitive commission rates, and excellent support. It also provides advanced analytics and reporting tools, making it easy for affiliates to track their performance and identify opportunities for improvement.

5. **ClickBank:** ClickBank is a well-established affiliate network that specializes in digital products, including ebooks, software, and courses. It offers a high commission rate and provides detailed analytics, making it easy for affiliates to track their performance and optimize their campaigns.

6. **FlexOffers:** FlexOffers is a rapidly growing affiliate network that offers a wide range of products and a competitive commission structure. It also provides advanced reporting and tracking tools, making it easy for affiliates to monitor their campaigns and optimize their performance.

Choosing the right affiliate network for your business can make a big difference in the success of your affiliate marketing efforts. Whether you're looking for a large network with a wide range of products, a network with a strong focus on analytics, or a network that specializes in a specific type of product, there is an affiliate network out there that can meet your needs. By doing your research and carefully considering your options, you can find the network that works best for you and your business.

Building Relationships with Merchants

It's a good idea to Build relationships with merchants in affiliate marketing as it can bring in higher commissions, unique promotions, and better product recommendations for your target audience. The key to building strong relationships with merchants is research and communication. Before approaching a merchant, ensure that their products align with your niche and target audience and that they have a good reputation. During communication, be professional, polite, and take the time to understand their needs and goals. Building a good relationship with merchants can not only increase your revenue, but it can also lead to long-term partnerships and growth opportunities for your affiliate marketing journey.

Additionally, staying up to date with the merchant's latest products and promotions can also help in maintaining a strong relationship. Being an active and engaged affiliate can show the merchant that you are invested in their success and are dedicated to promoting their products.

It's also important to provide valuable insights and feedback to the merchant about your audience and their buying behavior. This information can help the merchant improve their products and promotions, which in turn can benefit your affiliate marketing business.

Another way to build relationships with merchants is to attend industry events and conferences. These events provide a platform for you to meet merchants, network, and discuss potential partnerships.

Building relationships with merchants is a useful component of affiliate marketing success. By researching the merchant, communicating professionally, staying updated, and providing valuable insights, you can create long-lasting partnerships that can benefit both you and the merchant.

Setting Marketing Goals and Objectives

It can be helpful to set marketing goals and objectives for creating a successful affiliate marketing strategy. These goals and objectives will guide your efforts, track your progress, and measure your success. Here are some tips to help you set meaningful goals and objectives for your affiliate marketing business:

1. **Determine Your Target Audience:** Understanding your target audience is crucial in setting relevant marketing goals and objectives. Consider their needs, interests, and behaviors to tailor your goals and objectives accordingly.

2. **Define Your Business Objectives:** Consider your overall business objectives and how affiliate marketing can support those objectives. This could include increasing brand recognition, driving website traffic, or generating revenue.

3. **Set Specific, Measurable, Achievable, Relevant, and Time-bound (SMART) Goals:** SMART goals are specific, measurable, achievable, relevant, and time-bound goals that will help you track your progress and measure your success. For example, "Increase website traffic by 20% in the next 6 months through affiliate marketing."

4. **Choose Key Performance Indicators (KPIs):** KPIs are metrics that you can use to track your progress towards your goals. For example, your KPI for increasing website traffic could be website visits or clicks on affiliate links.

5. **Regularly Review and Revise Your Goals and Objectives:** Regularly reviewing your goals and objectives will help you make any necessary adjustments to stay on track and achieve your goals.

Setting marketing goals and objectives is an important step in creating a successful affiliate marketing strategy. By determining your target audience, defining your business objectives, setting SMART goals, choosing KPIs, and regularly reviewing and revising your goals, you can stay focused, track your progress, and measure your success.

Creating Content for Affiliate Marketing

The Importance of Content in Affiliate Marketing

The importance of content in affiliate marketing cannot be overstated. It is a crucial component that greatly contributes to the success of an affiliate marketing campaign. Whether you are a new affiliate marketer or an experienced one, having a strong content strategy can make all the difference in the success of your campaign.

Building trust with your target audience is critical in affiliate marketing. High-quality, relevant, and valuable content can help establish trust and credibility with your audience. By providing helpful information and addressing their needs and concerns, you can establish yourself as an expert in your niche and create a positive impression on your target audience. This is essential in building long-term customer loyalty and increasing conversion rates.

Establishing authority in your niche is another important aspect of content in affiliate marketing. By consistently creating high-quality, relevant, and valuable content, you can demonstrate your expertise and establish yourself as an authority in your niche. This can help you attract more customers and build a stronger brand reputation.

Additionally, quality content is essential for driving conversions in affiliate marketing. By providing valuable information, you are not only building trust and establishing authority, but also helping to guide your audience towards making a purchasing decision. Your content should be optimized for search engines and use keywords and phrases relevant to your niche to help your audience find you easily.

Content is a crucial element of affiliate marketing. By investing in a strong content strategy, you can build trust, establish authority, and drive conversions in your affiliate marketing campaign. Whether you are writing blog posts, creating videos, or developing other types of content, your focus should always be on providing value to your target audience. By doing so, you will be well on your way to success in the world of affiliate marketing.

Types of Content for Affiliate Marketing

As an affiliate marketer, there are various types of content you can use to promote your affiliate products and drive conversions. Choosing the right type of content to use can be a challenge, but by understanding your target audience and their preferences, you can make an informed decision.

Blog Posts: Blogging is a popular and effective form of content for affiliate marketers. By writing blog posts, you can provide valuable information and educate your audience on the products and services you are promoting. Your blog posts should be optimized for search engines and include relevant keywords and phrases to help your target audience find you easily.

Videos: Video content is another popular form of content for affiliate marketers. By creating engaging and informative videos, you can demonstrate the benefits of the products and services you are promoting and provide a more interactive experience for your audience.

Infographics: Infographics are a visual representation of information and data. They can be a great way to provide valuable information to your audience in a format that is both informative and engaging.

Social Media Posts: Social media platforms such as Twitter, Facebook, and Instagram are powerful tools for affiliate marketers. By sharing informative and engaging posts on these platforms, you can reach a large audience and drive traffic to your affiliate products.

Emails: Email marketing is a highly effective way to promote affiliate products. By sending targeted and personalized emails to your subscribers, you can provide valuable information, build relationships, and drive conversions.

Ebooks: Ebooks are a great way to provide in-depth information and educate your audience on a particular topic. By offering an ebook as a lead magnet, you can attract potential customers and provide them with valuable information on your niche.

Podcasts: Podcasts are a great way to reach a large audience and provide valuable information on your niche. By creating engaging and informative podcasts, you can build relationships with your audience and drive traffic to your affiliate products.

Product reviews: Write in-depth reviews of the products you're promoting as an affiliate. Be honest and provide your opinion about the product, along with any pros and cons.

How-to guides: Create step-by-step guides that demonstrate how to use the products you're promoting.

Listicles: Create list-style articles that highlight the top benefits or features of the products you're promoting.

There are many different types of content that can be used in affiliate marketing. By understanding your target audience and their preferences, you can choose the right type of content to use and effectively promote your affiliate products. Whether you prefer to use blog posts, videos, infographics, social media posts, emails, ebooks, or podcasts, the key is to provide valuable information and build relationships with your target audience.

Creating Quality Content that Converts

You can have the best and most well-informed content in the world, but it needs to convert to sales if you're going to succeed. The right content can help you build trust with your audience, increase engagement, and ultimately drive more sales. Here's a list of what you need to know to create content that will help you reach your affiliate marketing goals.

- **Find the Right Format:** Different types of content work better for different audiences. For example, a blog post might work well for one audience, while a video might be more effective for another. Experiment with different formats to see what works best for your target audience.

- **Provide Value:** The best affiliate marketing content provides value to the reader. This could be in the form of helpful tips, product reviews, or educational resources. The goal is to provide information that the reader can use to make informed decisions about the products you're promoting.

- **Focus on Quality:** Poor quality content can harm your credibility and reduce the chances of conversions. Make sure that your content is well-researched, well-written, and engaging.

- **Optimize for Search Engines:** Search engine optimization (SEO) can help you reach a wider audience. Use keywords, meta descriptions, and other tactics to improve your content's visibility in search results.

- **Promote Your Content:** Once your content is published, it's important to promote it to reach as many people as possible. Share it on social media, reach out to influencers in your niche, and consider running ads to drive traffic to your site.

Creating quality content is a critical part of any successful affiliate marketing strategy. By focusing on your target audience, providing value, and promoting your content, you can create content that converts and drives sales.

Optimizing Content for Search Engines

Whether it's your website, podcast, YouTube video, or social media channels, making sure your content is search engine optimized (SEO) will help you reach a wider audience, increase your visibility, and drive more traffic to your affiliate links. Here's why it's so important.

First and foremost, search engines like Google, Bing, and Yahoo are how most people find what they're looking for online. If you're not showing up in their search results, you're missing out on a lot of potential traffic and income. By optimizing your content for search engines, you can increase your chances of appearing in front of potential customers when they're searching for products or services related to your niche.

Another benefit of SEO is that it can help you establish yourself as an authority in your niche. When you consistently create high-quality, keyword-rich content that provides value to your audience, search engines will start to recognize your site as a reputable source of information. This will increase your search engine rankings and help you build a strong online presence over time.

When optimizing your content, there are several key factors to keep in mind. First, it's important to choose keywords and phrases that accurately reflect the content of your pages and blog posts. These keywords should be relevant to your niche and related to the products or services you're promoting.

Next, make sure your website is well-structured and easy to navigate. Use headings, subheadings, and bullet points to break up your content into digestible chunks, and make sure each page has a clear call to action that encourages visitors to take the next step, whether that's signing up for your newsletter, making a purchase, or visiting another page on your site.

Another important aspect of SEO is link building. This involves getting other websites to link to your pages and blog posts. Search engines see links as a "vote of confidence" for your content, so the more links you have pointing to your site, the higher your search engine rankings will be. You can build links by writing guest posts on other blogs, participating in online forums and discussion boards, and reaching out to other websites in your niche to request links.

Finally, make sure your website is mobile-friendly. More and more people are using their smartphones and tablets to search for products and services online, so it's essential that your site is optimized for mobile devices. This means using a responsive design that adjusts to the size of the screen, making sure your pages load quickly, and avoiding the use of Flash or other technologies that are not compatible with mobile devices.

Optimizing your content for search engines is an essential part of building a successful affiliate marketing business. By focusing on SEO best practices, you can reach more potential customers, establish yourself as an authority in your niche, and drive more traffic to your affiliate links.

Promoting Affiliate Products

Best Practices for Affiliate Promotion

Affiliate marketing is a great way to make money online by promoting other people's products. However, in order to be successful and maximize your earnings, it's important to follow best practices for affiliate promotion. Here are a few key tips to help you succeed:

- **Provide value to your audience:** Your focus should always be providing value to your audience. Offer them helpful tips, tutorials, and reviews about the products you promote. This will not only help you build trust with your audience, but it will also increase the chances of them making a purchase.

- **Use clear and concise language:** When promoting products, make sure to use clear and concise language. Avoid using hype or misleading statements that may turn off your audience.

- **Don't promote too many products at once:** Overloading your audience with too many products can be overwhelming. Focus on promoting a few high-quality products that you believe in and that you know your audience will love.

- **Test and track your results:** Keep track of which promotions and products are performing well. This will help you make better decisions in the future and optimize your affiliate marketing strategy.

By following these best practices for affiliate promotion, you can maximize your earnings and build a successful affiliate marketing business.

Utilizing Social Media for Affiliate Marketing

Social media has become a powerful tool for businesses of all sizes and industries, including affiliate marketing. By leveraging social media platforms, affiliate marketers can reach a large and diverse audience, build brand awareness, and promote their affiliate products effectively.

One of the key benefits of social media for affiliate marketers is the ability to target specific demographics and interests. For example, if you are promoting a fitness product, you can target individuals who follow fitness influencers, belong to fitness groups, or have shown interest in fitness products on their social media profiles. This way, you reach the right audience and increase the chances of conversions.

In addition to targeting specific audiences, social media also allows affiliate marketers to engage with their followers, build relationships, and establish trust. By posting regular, relevant, and valuable content, affiliate marketers can create a loyal following and increase brand awareness. For example, you can share blog posts, tutorials, testimonials, or behind-the-scenes content to provide value to your followers and demonstrate your expertise in your niche.

Moreover, social media also provides affiliate marketers with a platform to promote their affiliate products in a subtle yet effective way. By incorporating affiliate links in your social media posts, you can drive traffic to your affiliate products and earn commissions from sales.

Lastly, social media analytics can provide affiliate marketers with valuable insights into the performance of their campaigns, audience behavior, and overall ROI. This information can help affiliate marketers make data-driven decisions and continuously improve their social media strategy.

Social media is an essential tool for affiliate marketers looking to reach a large and engaged audience, build relationships, promote products, and track results. Whether you choose to use Facebook, Instagram, Twitter, LinkedIn, or any other platform, the key is to be consistent, relevant, and valuable in your approach.

Paid Advertising for Affiliate Marketing

Paid advertising is a powerful tool in the affiliate marketing arsenal that can help boost exposure, generate leads, and drive sales for your affiliate business. It's important to understand that paid advertising is not a silver bullet and must be used in conjunction with other marketing efforts to be effective.

To get started with paid advertising for your affiliate marketing business, you first need to identify your target audience like we talked about in previous chapters. This includes demographics such as age, gender, location, interests, and behaviors. With this information, you can choose the platforms that your target audience is most active on and begin creating advertising campaigns that reach them.

Next, you need to decide on the type of advertising you want to run. This could include paid search ads, display ads, social media ads, or video ads. Each type of advertising has its own set of strengths and weaknesses, and the one that is right for you will depend on your target audience, budget, and marketing goals.

Once you have chosen your advertising platform and type, you need to craft your ad campaigns. This includes writing compelling ad copy, selecting eye-catching images or videos, and setting your budget. It's important to remember that your ad campaigns must be optimized to drive conversions, so you need to be diligent in tracking and analyzing your results.

Another important factor to consider when running paid advertising campaigns is your landing page. This is the page that users will land on after clicking on your ad. It must be optimized for conversions, with a clear call to action and relevant information about the product you are promoting.

Finally, you need to have a plan for scaling your advertising efforts. This includes constantly testing and optimizing your ad campaigns, as well as experimenting with new advertising platforms and types. By continually refining your approach, you can ensure that your paid advertising efforts are driving the best possible results for your affiliate marketing business.

Paid advertising can be a highly effective tool for affiliate marketers looking to increase their visibility, drive leads, and generate sales. However, it requires careful planning, execution, and optimization to be successful. By following the tips outlined in this section, you can get started with your own successful paid advertising campaigns and reap the benefits of affiliate marketing.

Here's a list of the top advertising platforms you can use to send all that lovely traffic to your affiliate links:

- **Google AdWords:** Google AdWords is the largest and most popular platform for paid advertising. It allows you to place ads on Google's search engine results pages (SERPs), as well as on partner websites that use the Google Display Network. AdWords is a powerful platform for targeting specific keywords, demographics, and geographic locations, making it a great option for affiliate marketers looking to reach specific audiences.

- **Facebook Ads:** Facebook is the largest social media platform in the world, with over 2 billion active users. This provides a huge potential audience for your ads, and Facebook's targeting options make it easy to reach the right people. With Facebook Ads, you can target users based on their interests, behaviors, and demographics, allowing you to reach a highly targeted audience.

- **Instagram Ads:** Instagram is quickly becoming one of the most popular social media platforms, and its visual-first format makes it a great platform for affiliate marketers looking to promote products or services. Instagram Ads allow you to reach a large and engaged audience, and the platform's targeting options make it easy to reach the right people.

- **Twitter Ads:** Twitter is another popular social media platform, with over 330 million active users. It is a fast-paced and highly engaged platform, making it a great option for affiliate marketers looking to reach a younger, tech-savvy audience. With Twitter Ads, you can target users based on keywords, interests, behaviors, and location, allowing you to reach the right people with your ads.

Each of these platforms has its own strengths and weaknesses, and the best platform for you will depend on your specific goals and target audience. However, by considering these four platforms, you can be sure to reach a large and engaged audience and achieve the best results for your affiliate marketing business.

Building an Email List for Affiliate Marketing

Email marketing can be very effective in an affiliate marketing strategy. Building an email list allows you to reach out to your target audience directly, keep them informed about new products and promotions, and build a relationship with them over time. In this section, we'll discuss why building an email list is important for affiliate marketing and how you can get started.

Email marketing is one of the most cost-effective ways to reach and engage your target audience. Unlike other forms of marketing, such as paid advertising, email marketing allows you to reach your audience directly, giving you complete control over the messaging and frequency of your campaigns. Furthermore, email marketing has a high return on investment (ROI), with some studies showing that for every $1 spent, the average ROI is $38.

In affiliate marketing, building an email list can help you promote products and generate more sales. By sending targeted, relevant emails to your subscribers, you can drive more traffic to your affiliate links and increase your chances of earning commissions.

Getting Started with Building an Email List

Building an email list takes time, effort, and planning. Here are the steps you need to take to get started:

1. **Choose an email marketing platform:** There are many email marketing platforms to choose from, such as Mailchimp, ConvertKit, and Aweber. Choose a platform that offers the features you need, such as automation, landing pages, and integration with your website or other tools.

2. **Create opt-in forms:** Opt-in forms are the tools you use to collect email addresses from your website visitors. You can create these forms using your email marketing platform or a tool such as Leadpages or OptinMonster.

3. **Offer an incentive:** In order to encourage people to sign up for your email list, offer them an incentive such as a discount, free e-book, or early access to a new product.

4. **Promote your email list:** Make sure your email list is prominently featured on your website, social media accounts, and other marketing channels. You can also use paid advertising to drive traffic to your opt-in forms.

5. **Segment your list:** Once you've built your email list, it's important to segment it based on interests, location, and other factors. This will help you send more targeted, relevant emails to your subscribers, increasing the chances that they will engage with your content and make a purchase.

Building an email list is a powerful part of any affiliate marketing strategy. By collecting email addresses and sending targeted, relevant emails, you can increase your chances of generating sales and earning commissions. So, get started today, and start building your email list!

Maximizing Affiliate Earnings

Understanding Commission Structures

Affiliate marketing is a performance-based marketing model that rewards affiliates for driving traffic and sales to a merchant's website. Commission structures are an important aspect of this model, as they determine the amount of money that affiliates earn for their efforts. In this section, we'll take a closer look at the various types of commission structures used in affiliate marketing and how they impact affiliates.

Pay-Per-Sale (PPS)

This is the most straightforward commission structure in affiliate marketing. Under this model, affiliates earn a commission for every sale they drive to the merchant's website. The commission rate varies depending on the product and the merchant, but it typically ranges from 5% to 20% of the sale price. This type of commission structure is ideal for affiliates who have a strong following and are confident in their ability to drive sales.

Pay-Per-Lead (PPL)

Under this commission structure, affiliates earn a commission for every lead they generate for the merchant. A lead is typically defined as a potential customer who has taken a specific action, such as filling out a form, signing up for a newsletter, or downloading a white paper. The commission rate for PPL is typically lower than PPS, but it provides affiliates with an opportunity to earn money even if they don't drive a sale.

Cost-Per-Action (CPA)

Under this commission structure, affiliates earn a commission for every specific action that a customer takes, such as making a purchase, downloading an app, or signing up for a service. The commission rate for CPA is typically higher than PPL but lower than PPS, as the merchant is only paying for a specific action, not a sale. This type of commission structure is ideal for affiliates who have a strong understanding of consumer behavior and can drive high-quality traffic to the merchant's site.

Recurring Commission

Under this commission structure, affiliates earn a commission for every sale they drive to the merchant's website and continue to earn that commission for as long as the customer remains a customer. This type of commission structure is ideal for affiliates who drive a high volume of sales and want to earn residual income from their efforts.

Understanding commission structures is an important part of being a successful affiliate marketer. By knowing the different types of commission structures and how they impact your earnings, you can make informed decisions about the products and merchants you promote and maximize your earning potential.

Tracking Affiliate Sales and Commissions

Tracking Affiliate Sales and Commissions is a very helpful part of Affiliate Marketing. It helps affiliate marketers to accurately monitor their earnings and identify areas for improvement in their marketing strategies. In this section, we will discuss the importance of tracking sales and commissions and how to do it effectively.

Why tracking is important:

- It helps you to determine the success of your campaigns. By tracking your sales, you can see which products are selling the best and which affiliate networks are generating the most revenue. This information can then be used to optimize your campaigns and improve your earnings.

- Helps in monitoring earnings accurately. Tracking your sales and commissions enables you to have a clear picture of how much you are earning from each sale. This helps you to accurately track your income and make informed decisions on how to allocate your marketing budget.

- Enables you to identify areas for improvement. By tracking your sales and commissions, you can see which products are not selling well and why. This information can be used to make changes to your marketing strategies and improve your earnings.

How to track sales and commissions:

- Use Affiliate Tracking Software. Affiliate Tracking Software is a tool that helps you to track your sales and commissions accurately. This software integrates with your affiliate network and tracks sales and commissions in real-time. It provides you with a dashboard that shows your earnings, sales, and commission data.

- Utilize Affiliate Network Reporting. Most affiliate networks provide detailed reporting on your sales and commissions. These reports include information on the products that have sold, the commissions earned, and the date of the sale. This information is crucial in determining the success of your campaigns and identifying areas for improvement.

- Monitor your sales and commission data regularly. Regular monitoring of your sales and commission data is essential in ensuring that you are earning the most from your affiliate marketing efforts. This information can be used to make informed decisions on how to optimize your campaigns and increase your earnings.

Tracking Affiliate Sales and Commissions helps you to determine the success of your campaigns, monitor your earnings accurately, and identify areas for improvement. By utilizing Affiliate Tracking Software, utilizing Affiliate Network Reporting, and monitoring your sales and commission data regularly, you can maximize your earnings from Affiliate Marketing.

Increasing Conversion Rates

As an affiliate marketer, one of the primary goals is to drive traffic to your website or landing pages and convert that traffic into sales or commissions. To do this, you need to focus on increasing conversion rates, which is the percentage of visitors who take the desired action on your site, such as making a purchase or filling out a form. Here are some strategies for increasing conversion rates in affiliate marketing:

1. **Optimize your website for conversions:** This includes having a clear and compelling call-to-action (CTA), a well-designed landing page, and a user-friendly website. Your website should be designed to effectively communicate the value of the product or service you are promoting and make it easy for visitors to take action.

2. **Personalize your marketing approach:** Personalizing your marketing messages based on the needs, interests, and behaviors of your target audience can help increase conversion rates. By tailoring your messages to the specific needs and interests of your audience, you can make your marketing more relevant and effective.

3. **Offer incentives:** Offering incentives, such as discounts, bonuses, or free trials, can increase the motivation of your visitors to take action. For example, you can offer a discount code to customers who make a purchase through your affiliate link or offer a free trial of a product or service to customers who sign up for your email list.

4. **Utilize customer reviews and testimonials:** Including customer reviews and testimonials on your website or in your marketing materials can help build trust with your audience and increase conversion rates. People are more likely to make a purchase when they can see that others have had positive experiences with the product or service.

5. **Conduct A/B testing:** A/B testing is a process of testing two different versions of a marketing element, such as a landing page or email, to see which one performs better. By conducting A/B tests, you can determine the best approach for increasing conversion rates and optimize your marketing efforts.

By implementing these strategies and continually experimenting and testing, you can increase your conversion rates as an affiliate marketer and maximize your earnings potential. With the right approach and a commitment to continuous improvement, you can achieve success in the competitive world of affiliate marketing.

Negotiating Higher Commissions

As an affiliate marketer, one of your main goals is to maximize your earnings and increase your commission rates. Negotiating higher commissions with merchants can be a great way to achieve this goal. However, it's important to approach negotiations in a professional and strategic way to increase your chances of success.

Understand your value: Before you start negotiating, it's important to understand the value you bring to the merchant. This includes the number of clicks and conversions you generate, your target audience, and any other factors that make your partnership valuable to the merchant. By understanding your value, you'll be better equipped to negotiate for higher commissions.

Know the merchant's goals: Before negotiating, research the merchant's goals and target audience. Understanding what the merchant is trying to achieve will give you a better idea of how you can help them reach their goals and why they should be willing to pay higher commissions.

Be prepared to compromise: Negotiating is a two-way street, so be prepared to compromise. If a merchant is unwilling to pay higher commissions, consider offering to promote their products more frequently or to a wider audience. By compromising, you can reach a mutually beneficial agreement that satisfies both parties.

Make your case: When negotiating, make a clear and concise case for why you deserve higher commissions. Explain how your efforts have increased the merchant's sales and how you plan to continue promoting their products in the future.

Be professional: Above all, it's important to approach negotiations in a professional and respectful manner. Being polite and respectful can help build a positive relationship with the merchant and increase your chances of success in future negotiations.

By following these tips, you can negotiate higher commissions and increase your earnings as an affiliate marketer. Remember, building strong relationships with merchants is key to success in affiliate marketing, so be patient and persistent in your negotiations.

Managing and Growing Your Affiliate Business

Measuring and Analyzing Performance

Measuring and analyzing performance is critical for affiliate marketers as it helps them to assess the effectiveness of their strategies and make necessary changes. This process enables affiliate marketers to identify areas of improvement, track the impact of their efforts, and ultimately increase their success.

One of the key metrics to track as an affiliate marketer is conversions. This includes the number of visitors to your website who take the desired action, such as making a purchase or filling out a form. By monitoring conversions, affiliate marketers can assess how well their efforts are resonating with their target audience and adjust as necessary.

Another important metric to track is revenue. This includes the amount of money generated from affiliate sales and commissions. Tracking revenue helps affiliate marketers to understand the financial impact of their efforts and make decisions about where to allocate resources for maximum return on investment.

Click-through rate (CTR) is also a crucial metric to track. CTR measures the number of clicks a specific affiliate link receives in relation to the number of times it is displayed. Tracking CTR helps affiliate marketers to assess the effectiveness of their promotions and adjust improve performance.

In addition to tracking key metrics, affiliate marketers should also analyze the performance of their campaigns and promotions. This can be done by reviewing the results of A/B testing, analyzing website traffic patterns, and evaluating the success of specific promotions. By understanding what is working and what isn't, affiliate marketers can make informed decisions about how to optimize their strategies for maximum success.

Ultimately, measuring and analyzing performance is an ongoing process that requires patience, persistence, and a commitment to continuous improvement. By staying focused on the metrics that matter and making data-driven decisions, affiliate marketers can increase their chances of success and achieve their goals.

Scaling Your Affiliate Marketing Business

Scaling an affiliate marketing business can take your income and success to the next level, but it requires careful planning and execution. Here are some key factors to consider when scaling your affiliate marketing business:

- **Diversifying Your Portfolio:** Don't rely too heavily on any one affiliate network or merchant. Consider adding more affiliate programs to your portfolio to reduce your risk and increase your earning potential.

- **Expanding Your Reach:** Find new ways to reach your target audience. This can include leveraging social media, building a blog, creating YouTube videos, and utilizing paid advertising.

- **Improving Your Conversion Rates:** Increase the rate at which you convert clicks into sales by optimizing your content, website, and landing pages. This can include split testing, A/B testing, and utilizing customer feedback.

- **Leveraging Automation:** Utilize tools and technologies to automate repetitive tasks, such as email marketing and affiliate link management. This will allow you to focus on high-impact tasks and scale your business more efficiently.

- **Networking with Other Affiliates:** Build relationships with other affiliates in your niche. This can help you learn from each other, cross-promote each other's products, and collaborate on joint ventures.

- **Continuously Improving:** Continuously analyze your performance, track your results, and make improvements to your strategy. This can include tracking metrics such as click-through rates, conversion rates, and revenue per visitor.

Scaling an affiliate marketing business is a marathon, not a sprint. It takes time, dedication, and effort to achieve your goals. Focus on creating a solid foundation, and continually strive to improve your performance and reach your target audience. With the right strategy, effort, and persistence, you can scale your affiliate marketing business to new heights.

Staying Up to Date with Industry Trends

Staying up to date with industry trends in affiliate marketing is important for staying ahead of the competition and maximizing your earnings. Affiliate marketing is a rapidly evolving industry and keeping abreast of the latest trends and developments is essential for staying relevant and growing your business.

One of the keyways to stay informed about the latest industry trends is to regularly attend affiliate marketing events and conferences. These events bring together experts from the industry to share their knowledge, experience and insights on the latest trends and best practices. Attending these events can provide you with valuable information on how to optimize your affiliate marketing efforts and increase your earnings.

Another way to stay informed about industry trends is to subscribe to relevant blogs and online forums. Many affiliate marketing experts publish regular articles and blog posts on the latest trends and best practices. By subscribing to these resources, you can stay informed about the latest developments in the industry and gain valuable insights into how to improve your affiliate marketing efforts.

Social media can also be a great source of information on industry trends. Many affiliate marketers use social media to share their experiences, opinions, and insights on the latest developments in the industry. Following the right influencers on social media can provide you with valuable information and insights that you can use to improve your affiliate marketing efforts.

Reading industry publications and trade magazines can also be a great way to stay informed about the latest trends and developments in affiliate marketing. Industry publications often provide in-depth analysis and reporting on the latest developments in the industry, giving you valuable insights into what is happening in the industry and what you need to do to stay ahead.

Finally, networking with other affiliate marketers is a great way to stay informed about industry trends. By connecting with other affiliate marketers, you can share ideas, discuss challenges, and gain valuable insights into the latest trends and best practices. Networking can also help you establish partnerships and collaborations that can help you grow your business.

Staying up to date with industry trends in affiliate marketing is crucial for maximizing your earnings and staying ahead of the competition. By attending events, subscribing to relevant resources, using social media, reading industry publications, and networking with other affiliate marketers, you can stay informed and grow your business.

Here's a list of useful blogs to stay abreast of what's going on in the world of affiliate marketing. There's a wealth of knowledge here as well as useful tools to help you succeed on your journey.

1. **Authority Hacker:** Authority Hacker is a blog that focuses on helping marketers grow their businesses through affiliate marketing, SEO, and content marketing. They offer a wealth of resources, including in-depth articles, tutorials, and courses.

2. **Smart Affiliate Success:** Smart Affiliate Success is a blog that provides tips, tricks, and strategies for making money through affiliate marketing. They cover a wide range of topics, including SEO, email marketing, and product selection.

3. **Affiliate Marketing Blog by Geno Prussakov:** Geno Prussakov's blog is a valuable resource for affiliate marketers of all levels. He covers a wide range of topics, including affiliate program management, marketing strategies, and affiliate network selection.

4. **Niche Hacks:** Niche Hacks is a blog that focuses on helping marketers find and exploit profitable niches through affiliate marketing. They provide a wealth of resources, including in-depth articles, case studies, and tools.

5. **Matthew Woodward:** Matthew Woodward is a successful affiliate marketer and blogger who shares his knowledge and insights on his blog. He covers a wide range of topics, including SEO, link building, and product promotion.

6. **Affiliate Tips:** Affiliate Tips is a blog that provides useful tips, tricks, and resources for affiliate marketers. They cover a wide range of topics, including product selection, marketing strategies, and network selection.

7. **Affiliate Marketing Mastery:** Affiliate Marketing Mastery is a blog that provides a comprehensive guide to affiliate marketing, including strategies, techniques, and tools. They cover a wide range of topics, including niche selection, product promotion, and conversion optimization.

Overcoming Challenges and Risks in Affiliate Marketing

Affiliate marketing is a popular and lucrative way to earn money online by promoting other people's products. However, like any business, it comes with its own set of challenges and risks that must be overcome in order to succeed. In this section, we'll look at some of the most common challenges and risks faced by affiliate marketers and offer some strategies for overcoming them.

One of the biggest challenges faced by affiliate marketers is finding the right products to promote. This requires research, testing, and analysis to ensure that the product you're promoting is in demand, of high quality, and likely to convert. To overcome this challenge, you need to have a solid understanding of your target market and the products they are most likely to buy. You can use tools such as keyword research, market research, and competitor analysis to find the right products to promote.

Another challenge is getting traffic to your affiliate marketing website. This requires a solid understanding of search engine optimization (SEO) and paid advertising. You need to be able to create high-quality, engaging content that is optimized for the search engines and designed to convert visitors into buyers. You also need to be able to drive traffic to your site using a combination of SEO, social media, and paid advertising.

One of the biggest risks in affiliate marketing is the risk of being banned by the merchant or the affiliate network. This can happen if you engage in spamming, unethical marketing practices, or violate the terms of the affiliate agreement. To avoid being banned, you need to be transparent in your marketing practices and comply with the terms of the affiliate agreement. You should also be honest and upfront about your intentions with the merchants and affiliate networks you work with.

Finally, one of the biggest challenges in affiliate marketing is dealing with the competition. There are many affiliate marketers out there competing for the same customers and products. To overcome this challenge, you need to be creative and innovative in your marketing strategies. You need to be able to stand out from the crowd by offering unique and valuable content, building strong relationships with your customers, and providing excellent customer service.

Affiliate marketing is a challenging but rewarding business. By overcoming the challenges and risks, you can create a successful and profitable affiliate marketing business. To be successful, you need to be diligent, strategic, and persistent in your efforts. You need to have a deep understanding of your target market, the products you're promoting, and the strategies that work best in your niche. With the right tools, knowledge, and attitude, you can overcome the challenges and risks of affiliate marketing and achieve great success.

The Future of Affiliate Marketing

The Impact of Technology on Affiliate Marketing

Technology has had a profound impact on the way we live and work, and the affiliate marketing industry is no exception. In recent years, technology has changed the way affiliate marketers approach their work and how they interact with merchants and customers. The introduction of new technologies and platforms has opened new opportunities for affiliate marketers and has made it easier for them to reach their target audience and increase conversions.

One of the biggest impacts of technology on affiliate marketing has been the growth of e-commerce. With more and more people shopping online, affiliate marketers have been able to tap into this growing market by promoting products and services through their websites and social media platforms. This has made it easier for affiliate marketers to reach a wider audience and increase their earning potential.

Another impact of technology on affiliate marketing has been the rise of mobile devices. With the increasing popularity of smartphones and tablets, affiliate marketers have been able to reach their target audience on the go. This has allowed them to promote products and services in real-time and engage with customers in new and innovative ways.

The rise of artificial intelligence and machine learning has also had a significant impact on affiliate marketing. By using these technologies, affiliate marketers can analyze vast amounts of data and gain a deeper understanding of their target audience and their purchasing habits. This can help affiliate marketers to make more informed decisions about which products to promote and how to reach their target audience more effectively. More on artificial intelligence later and how it can aid your marketing efforts.

Finally, the increasing popularity of social media has had a major impact on affiliate marketing. Social media platforms have made it easier for affiliate marketers to connect with their target audience and promote products and services in a more engaging and interactive way. By leveraging the power of social media, affiliate marketers can build relationships with their target audience, increase brand awareness, and ultimately, drive more conversions.

The impact of technology on affiliate marketing has been profound and far-reaching. With the continued development of new technologies and platforms, affiliate marketers have been able to reach their target audience in new and innovative ways and increase their earning potential. As the industry continues to evolve, affiliate marketers must stay up to date with the latest trends and technologies in order to stay ahead of the curve and succeed in this highly competitive field.

The Rise of Influencer Marketing

Influencer marketing has been on the rise in recent years and has become an increasingly popular marketing strategy, not just in affiliate marketing but in the marketing industry as a whole. The idea behind influencer marketing is to leverage the influence that individuals with a large following on social media platforms have over their followers to promote a product or service. In this section, we will look at the rise of influencer marketing in affiliate marketing and why it has become so popular.

The rise of influencer marketing can be attributed to the increased use of social media platforms by consumers and businesses alike. With billions of active users on social media, it has become a prime location for companies to reach potential customers and promote their products or services. The power of social media lies in the ability of influencers to reach a large number of people in a short amount of time and build trust with their followers. This makes influencer marketing an attractive option for companies looking to expand their reach and increase their sales.

In affiliate marketing, influencer marketing has proven to be an effective way to drive traffic and sales to a merchant's website. Influencers can promote a product or service by creating content that highlights its benefits and uses, such as a review or a demonstration video. This type of content can reach a large audience and help to build trust with potential customers. Additionally, influencer marketing can be a cost-effective way for merchants to reach their target audience, as influencers often charge lower fees compared to traditional forms of advertising.

Another reason for the rise of influencer marketing in affiliate marketing is the growing popularity of influencer networks. These networks connect merchants with influencers, making it easier for merchants to find the right influencer for their product or service. This can be especially helpful for smaller businesses, which may not have the resources to build relationships with individual influencers on their own. Influencer networks can also help to track and measure the success of an influencer campaign, providing merchants with valuable insights into their target audience and the effectiveness of their marketing efforts.

The rise of influencer marketing in affiliate marketing is a result of the growing popularity of social media, the cost-effectiveness of influencer marketing, and the availability of influencer networks. Whether you are a merchant or an affiliate marketer, it is important to understand the power of influencer marketing and to explore the opportunities that it presents. By leveraging the influence of influencers, you can reach a large audience and drive sales, making it a valuable tool in your affiliate marketing strategy.

Artificial Intelligence and Affiliate Marketing

Artificial Intelligence (AI) has revolutionized many industries, and affiliate marketing is no exception. AI has the potential to greatly enhance the performance and effectiveness of affiliate marketing campaigns, by automating repetitive tasks, optimizing conversion rates, and providing valuable insights into consumer behavior.

One of the key benefits of AI in affiliate marketing is the ability to automate repetitive tasks such as keyword research, bid management, and optimization of ad copy. AI algorithms can analyze large amounts of data, identify trends and patterns, and adjust campaigns in real-time to maximize ROI.

Another benefit of AI in affiliate marketing is the ability to optimize conversion rates. AI algorithms can analyze consumer behavior data, such as click-through rates, time on site, and conversion rates, and use this information to make data-driven decisions about which offers to promote, which ad copy to use, and which landing pages to send traffic to.

AI can also provide valuable insights into consumer behavior and help affiliate marketers better understand their target audience. AI algorithms can analyze large amounts of data, such as social media behavior, website activity, and purchase history, to identify consumer preferences, needs, and buying habits. This information can then be used to personalize the affiliate marketing experience and deliver more relevant offers to consumers.

The use of AI in affiliate marketing has the potential to greatly enhance the performance and effectiveness of affiliate marketing campaigns. From automating repetitive tasks, to optimizing conversion rates, and providing valuable insights into consumer behavior, AI has the potential to revolutionize the affiliate marketing industry. As AI technology continues to evolve, it is likely that we will see even more innovative applications of AI in affiliate marketing in the future.

Bonus Chapter - Utilizing Artificial Intelligence in Affiliate Marketing

Artificial Intelligence has been playing an ever-increasing role in the world of affiliate marketing in the last few years. At the time of writing this book, this role is rapidly moving to the next level. With the release of things like OpenAI's ChatGPT that has been made open to the public and free to use, it's prompted a mass adoption across many different industries and affiliate marketing is no exception.

With this in mind, I've decided to add an extra bonus chapter covering exactly this phenomenon and how you can use it to your advantage. Platforms like ChatGPT are just the beginning. Soon there will no doubt be all manner of different powerful AI tools to choose from such as Google's Bard that's currently racing to market in an attempt to rival ChatGPT. There's a lot to consider when it comes to artificial intelligence but in this chapter, we'll focus on how it can aid you in your affiliate marketing efforts going forward. It's an exciting time to be in the world of online marketing and these new powerful AI tools will surely make our lives a lot easier, our strategies more efficient and our analysis data a lot more useful. So, let's jump in and embrace it!

Utilizing AI for Keyword Research and Target Audience Analysis

Affiliate marketing is a rapidly growing industry, and with the rise of technology, there has been a shift towards using artificial intelligence (AI) to help improve marketing efforts. One of the areas where AI can be especially useful is in keyword research and target audience analysis. Here are some ways that AI can be utilized in these areas to help affiliate marketers achieve success.

Keyword Research

One of the most important aspects of affiliate marketing is finding the right keywords to target in your marketing efforts. AI can help in this regard by using machine learning algorithms to analyze large amounts of data and determine which keywords are likely to be the most effective for your marketing campaign.

For example, AI can analyze search engine data to determine which keywords are being searched for the most, and which ones have the highest conversion rates. It can also analyze your competitors' websites to determine which keywords they are targeting, and what makes their campaigns successful.

Target Audience Analysis

Another area where AI can be helpful is in target audience analysis. This involves using data to determine who your target audience is, what their interests are, and how you can reach them. AI can analyze large amounts of data, such as social media and website data, to determine what types of content your target audience is engaging with, and what their interests are.

For example, AI can analyze your target audience's social media activity to determine which topics they are interested in, and what types of content they are most likely to engage with. This information can then be used to create targeted campaigns that are more likely to convert.

AI can play a critical role in helping affiliate marketers achieve success. By utilizing AI for keyword research and target audience analysis, marketers can gain a better understanding of their target audience and create more effective campaigns. Whether you are just starting out in affiliate marketing or are an experienced marketer, using AI can help you achieve better results and maximize your earning potential.

Implementing AI Chatbots for Customer Engagement and Sales Conversion

Artificial intelligence (AI) has revolutionized various industries, including the lucrative world of affiliate marketing. One of the key areas where AI has made a significant impact is customer engagement and sales conversion. By using AI chatbots, affiliate marketers can effectively engage with their target audience and drive conversions.

Chatbots are computer programs designed to mimic human conversations. They can be integrated into websites, messaging platforms, and mobile apps, providing customers with instant and personalized support. AI chatbots use machine learning algorithms to understand and respond to customer queries in real-time, making them an ideal tool for affiliate marketers looking to improve customer engagement and conversion rates.

There are several benefits to using AI chatbots in affiliate marketing, including:

- **24/7 Availability:** AI chatbots are available 24/7, meaning that customers can get support and make purchases at any time of day or night. This is particularly important for affiliate marketers targeting global audiences, as customers in different time zones can receive support when they need it.

- **Personalized Support:** AI chatbots use machine learning algorithms to understand customer queries and provide personalized support. This helps to build a stronger relationship with customers and increase the likelihood of conversions.

- **Increased Productivity:** AI chatbots can handle a large volume of customer queries and support requests simultaneously, freeing up time for affiliate marketers to focus on other aspects of their business.

- **Improved Customer Experience:** By providing instant and personalized support, AI chatbots help to improve the customer experience and increase customer satisfaction. This can lead to repeat purchases and higher conversion rates.

- **Data Collection and Analysis:** AI chatbots collect data on customer interactions, which can be used to analyze customer behavior and preferences. This information can then be used to optimize the customer journey and improve conversion rates.

Implementing an AI chatbot for customer engagement and sales conversion in affiliate marketing is relatively straightforward. There are several AI chatbot platforms available, many of which offer drag-and-drop interfaces and pre-built templates. This makes it easy for affiliate marketers to create and customize their own chatbots, without the need for extensive technical knowledge.

AI chatbots are a powerful tool for affiliate marketers looking to improve customer engagement and drive conversions. By providing instant and personalized support, AI chatbots help to build stronger relationships with customers, increase customer satisfaction, and optimize the customer journey.

Here's a list of the best AI chatbots around at the moment you can implement into your website and supercharge your marketing strategy.

1. **MobileMonkey:** MobileMonkey is a powerful AI chatbot that helps businesses increase sales and engagement with their customers. It offers a variety of features, including personalized product recommendations, cart recovery, and lead generation.

2. **Tars:** Tars is an AI chatbot builder that helps businesses create custom chatbots for their websites and messaging platforms. With Tars, you can automate customer support, provide personalized recommendations, and increase conversions.

3. **ManyChat:** ManyChat is an AI chatbot platform that helps businesses engage with their customers on messaging platforms such as Facebook Messenger. With ManyChat, you can automate customer support, provide personalized product recommendations, and collect lead information.

4. **Chatfuel:** Chatfuel is an AI chatbot builder that helps businesses create custom chatbots for their websites and messaging platforms. With Chatfuel, you can automate customer support, provide personalized product recommendations, and increase conversions.

5. **SnatchBot:** SnatchBot is a powerful AI chatbot platform that helps businesses automate customer support, increase conversions, and improve customer engagement. With SnatchBot, you can create custom chatbots, provide personalized recommendations, and collect lead information.

These AI chatbots are easy to use and can help you increase conversions and engagement with your customers, making them a valuable tool for affiliate marketers. By incorporating AI chatbots into your affiliate marketing strategy, you can improve your customer experience and maximize your earnings.

Using Artificial Intelligence for Content Creation

Artificial intelligence has the potential to revolutionize content creation for affiliate marketers. AI technology has come a long way in recent years and can now help to automate and streamline various aspects of content creation. This can be particularly useful for affiliate marketers who are looking to maximize their profits and reach a wider audience.

One way that AI can help with content creation is by automating the research process. AI algorithms can quickly gather data from various sources and use this information to inform the creation of content. For example, AI can help to identify keywords and phrases that are most relevant to a particular niche or audience. This information can then be used to optimize content for search engines, making it more likely that your content will be discovered by potential customers.

Another way that AI can help with content creation is by generating original content. AI algorithms can use data from a variety of sources to create new content that is both informative and engaging. This can include anything from blog posts and articles to social media posts and product descriptions. AI technology can even be used to create images and videos, which can be particularly useful for affiliate marketers who want to add a visual component to their content.

Finally, AI can help with content creation by analyzing the performance of existing content. This can include tracking metrics such as views, clicks, and conversions, and using this data to optimize content and improve overall performance. For example, AI algorithms can analyze data to determine which keywords and topics are most effective in driving traffic and conversions and use this information to inform future content creation.

AI technology has the potential to greatly enhance content creation for affiliate marketers. Whether you're looking to automate the research process, generate original content, or analyze the performance of existing content, AI has a lot to offer. By leveraging AI, affiliate marketers can increase the effectiveness of their content and reach a wider audience, ultimately helping to maximize their profits and achieve greater success.

The Future of AI in Affiliate Marketing: Opportunities and Challenges

The use of artificial intelligence (AI) in affiliate marketing is becoming more and more popular, with many marketers exploring the potential benefits it can bring to their business. From keyword research and target audience analysis to customer engagement and sales conversion, AI has the potential to revolutionize the way affiliate marketing is done.

However, as with any new technology, there are also potential challenges and risks that must be considered. This section will explore the future of AI in affiliate marketing, including both the opportunities and the challenges that this rapidly evolving field presents.

Opportunities

As previously mentioned, one of the biggest opportunities that AI presents to affiliate marketers is the ability to automate many of the time-consuming and repetitive tasks that are required to run a successful marketing campaign. From keyword research and competitor analysis to customer engagement and lead generation, AI-powered tools can help to streamline the process and free up time for more strategic work.

Another opportunity that AI presents is the ability to access and analyze large amounts of data in real-time, providing affiliate marketers with valuable insights into customer behavior and preferences. By utilizing AI tools, marketers can gain a deeper understanding of their target audience and craft more effective campaigns that resonate with their customers.

Challenges

Despite the many benefits that AI can bring to affiliate marketing, there are also significant challenges that must be addressed. One of the biggest challenges is the risk of relying too heavily on AI and neglecting the human element that is essential to effective marketing. While AI tools can help to automate and streamline certain tasks, it is still essential for affiliate marketers to understand the motivations and desires of their target audience, and to be able to connect with them on a human level.

Another challenge that AI presents is the potential for bias. AI algorithms are only as good as the data they are trained on, and if the data contains biases, these biases can be reflected in the results. It is important for affiliate marketers to be aware of the potential for bias and to work to address it in their AI tools and algorithms.

The future of AI in affiliate marketing is both exciting and uncertain. While there are many opportunities to automate and streamline tasks, and to access valuable customer insights, there are also significant challenges that must be addressed. As affiliate marketers embrace the power of AI, it is important to balance the benefits with the risks, and to carefully consider the role that this technology will play in their marketing strategy.

Conclusion

Well, there you have it. That's affiliate marketing in a nutshell. A rather large nutshell albeit, but a nutshell all the same. I tried to keep this book relatively short and concise as not to overwhelm. I tried to avoid waffle as much as possible as well, since time is precious and actually taking action is important. Well, it's more than important, it's imperative! And this book should have armed you with the knowledge you need to get started on your own exciting affiliate marketing journey.

Growing an affiliate marketing business can be a challenging but rewarding journey. With the right knowledge, strategies and tactics, anyone can successfully build an affiliate marketing empire. Moreover, incorporating artificial intelligence into your marketing efforts can bring significant advantages to your business, from automating routine tasks to increasing your conversion rates. AI chatbots are a great example of how technology can make a difference in the affiliate marketing industry.

In this book, we covered the basics of affiliate marketing, from how to get started to how to find and join affiliate programs. We also discussed how to select the right products and niches, how to promote your affiliate products effectively, and how to measure and optimize your performance. Finally, we looked at how AI can help you grow your affiliate marketing business, from customer engagement and lead generation to sales and customer support.

I hope that the information and insights shared in this book will help you build a successful and profitable affiliate marketing business. Whether you are a beginner or an experienced marketer, you now have the tools and knowledge to take your affiliate marketing efforts to the next level!

I would like to thank you for taking the time to read this book and for your interest in affiliate marketing. It's the entrepreneurially minded individuals like yourself that I really admire. Doing whatever it takes to build the life you want and on YOUR terms. It takes bags of courage, motivation, patience, persistence and defiantly a few sleepless nights but once you get there, it will all be worth it. I sincerely wish you all the best in your journey and hope that you will share your success stories with me one day. Happy affiliate marketing!

-   *Will Strong*